FAMILY PRAYER

CHARLES MICHAEL

Gifted Books and Media

Copyright

Paperback ISBN: 978-1-947343-21-4
Published by Jayclad Publishing LLC
www.giftedbookstore.com

Table of Contents

How to Use this Book

- The prayers given in this book is one continuous prayer. It begins with praise and ends with petition prayer (followed by Rosary and Bible Reading).

- Families must spend at least 30 minutes in prayer each day.

- The first time, you use this book, read the notes about each section of the prayer. Why we should forgive or why we should repent before placing our petitions to God is mentioned in the second part of this book.

- Pray in the order given in the book. For example, it is important that we begin with praise and worship because it is the biblical way. We enter God's presence through praising him (Ps 100:4, Ps 22:3).

- For each line of prayer, one person says the intention and the rest of the family members respond with the other half of the intention. For example, In this line of prayer, "Abba Father, you are almighty, ... I praise and worship you.", one person says, "Abba Father, you are almighty", and the rest of the family members respond with "I Praise and Adore you".

- When possible, parents must also take children to Daily Mass during holidays.

- Parents must also take children to regular confessions.

- This book is also available as an app in the Appstore for Apple users. Visit our website www.giftedbookstore.com for more information.

Part 1

Family Prayer

Praise and Worship

Abba Father, you are almighty, ... *I praise and worship you*
Abba Father, you are sovereign, ... *I praise and worship you*
Abba Father, you are all-powerful, ... *I praise and worship you*
Abba Father, you are all-knowing, ... *I praise and worship you*
Abba Father, you are Holy, ... *I praise and worship you*
Abba Father, you are the righteous one, ... *I praise and worship you*
Abba Father, you are eternal, ... *I praise and worship you*
Abba Father, you are Spirit and truth, ... *I praise and worship you*
Abba Father, you are God Most High, ... *I praise and worship you*
Abba Father, you are Lord of Hosts, ... *I praise and worship you*
Abba Father, you are the Great IAM, ... *I praise and worship you*
Abba Father, Lord of heaven and earth, ... *I praise and worship you*
Abba Father, you are loving, ... *I praise and worship you*
Abba Father, you are merciful, ... *I praise and worship you*
Abba Father, you are compassionate, ... *I praise and worship you*
Abba Father, you are patient, ... *I praise and worship you*
Abba Father, you are kind, ... *I praise and worship you*
Abba Father, you are generous, ... *I praise and worship you*
Abba Father, you are faithful, ... *I praise and worship you*
Abba Father, you are trustworthy, ... *I praise and worship you*
Abba Father, you are the truth, ... *I praise and worship you*
Abba Father, you are perfect, ... *I praise and worship you*
Abba Father, you are slow to anger, ... *I praise and worship you*
Abba Father, you are gracious, ... *I praise and worship you*
Abba Father, you are full of wisdom, ... *I praise and worship you*
Abba Father, you are a living God, ... *I praise and worship you*

Jesus, you are the good shepherd, ... *I praise and worship you*

Jesus, you are the truth, ... *I praise and worship you*

Jesus, you are the way, ... *I praise and worship you*

Jesus, you are the life, ...*I praise and worship you*

Jesus, you are the resurrection, ... *I praise and worship you*

Jesus, you are the healer, ... *I praise and worship you*

Jesus, you are the deliverer, ... *I praise and worship you*

Jesus, you are the anointed one, ... *I praise and worship you*

Jesus, you are the holy one, ... *I praise and worship you*

Jesus, you are the light of the world, ... *I praise and worship you*

Jesus, you are meek and humble, ... *I praise and worship you*

Jesus, you are the son of God, ... *I praise and worship you*

Jesus, you are seated at the right hand of the Father, ... *I praise and worship you*

Jesus, you are the Alpha and Omega, ... *I praise and worship you*

Jesus, you are the prince of peace, ... *I praise and worship you*

Jesus, you are the righteous one, ... *I praise and worship you*

Jesus, you are the comforter of the afflicted, ... *I praise and worship you*

Jesus, you are the consoler of the wounded, ... *I praise and worship you*

Jesus, you are the savior of the world, ... *I praise and worship you*

Jesus, you are the redeemer of mankind, ... *I praise and worship you*

Jesus, you are the wonderful counselor, ... *I praise and worship you*

Jesus, you are the true bread, ... *I praise and worship you*

Jesus, you are the bread from heaven, ... *I praise and worship you*

Jesus, you are the living Word, ... *I praise and worship you*

Jesus, you are the Word made flesh, ... *I praise and worship you*

Jesus, you are the Word of God, ... *I praise and worship you*

Jesus, you are the second person of the trinity, ... *I praise and worship you*

Jesus, you are the power of God, ... *I praise and worship you*

Jesus, you are the king of kings and Lord of lords, ... *I praise and worship you*

Jesus, you are the lamb of God, ... *I praise and worship you*
Jesus, you are the author of life, ... *I praise and worship you*
Jesus, you are the friend of sinners, ... *I praise and worship you*
Jesus, you are the atoning sacrifice, ... *I praise and worship you*
Jesus, you have the words of eternal life, ... *I praise and worship you*

Holy Spirit, ... *I praise and worship you*
Spirit of Abba Father, ... *I praise and worship you*
Spirit of Christ, ... *I praise and worship you*
Spirit of God, ... *I praise and worship you*
Spirit of the Lord, ... *I praise and worship you*
Holy Spirit, the Lord, ... *I praise and worship you*
Holy Spirit, power of the Most High, ... *I praise and worship you*
Spirit of the living God, ... *I praise and worship you*
Spirit of divinity, ... *I praise and worship you*
Breadth of the Almighty, ... *I praise and worship you*
Eternal Spirit, ... *I praise and worship you*
Spirit of the Son, ... *I praise and worship you*
Spirit of love, ... *I praise and worship you*
Spirit of joy, ... *I praise and worship you*
Spirit of peace, ... *I praise and worship you*
Spirit of kindness, ... *I praise and worship you*
Spirit of faithfulness, ... *I praise and worship you*
Spirit of gentleness, ... *I praise and worship you*
Spirit of self-control, ... *I praise and worship you*
Spirit of patience, ... *I praise and worship you*
Spirit of generosity, ... *I praise and worship you*
Spirit of modesty, ... *I praise and worship you*
Spirit of chastity, ... *I praise and worship you*
Spirit of goodness, ... *I praise and worship you*
Spirit of knowledge, ... *I praise and worship you*
Spirit of wisdom, ... *I praise and worship you*
Spirit of understanding, ... *I praise and worship you*

Spirit of fortitude, ... *I praise and worship you*
Spirit of counsel, ... *I praise and worship you*
Spirit of piety, ... *I praise and worship you*
Spirit of fear of God, ... *I praise and worship you*
Spirit of word of wisdom, ... *I praise and worship you*
Spirit of word of knowledge, ... *I praise and worship you*
Spirit of prophecy, ... *I praise and worship you*
Spirit of healing, ... *I praise and worship you*
Spirit of miracles, ... *I praise and worship you*
Spirit of discernment, ... *I praise and worship you*
Spirit of faith, ... *I praise and worship you*
Spirit of tongues, ... *I praise and worship you*
Spirit of interpretation of tongues, ... *I praise and worship you*
Spirit of truth, ... *I praise and worship you*
Spirit of righteousness, ... *I praise and worship you*
Spirit of glory, ... *I praise and worship you*
Spirit of grace, ... *I praise and worship you*
Spirit of holiness, ... *I praise and worship you*
Spirit of revelation, ... *I praise and worship you*
Spirit of life, ... *I praise and worship you*
Spirit of Justice, ... *I praise and worship you*
Water of life, ... *I praise and worship you*
Holy Spirit, the helper, ... *I praise and worship you*
Holy Spirit, the advocate, ... *I praise and worship you*
Holy Spirit, the guide, ... *I praise and worship you*
Holy Spirit, the Comforter, ... *I praise and worship you*
Holy Spirit, the counselor, ... *I praise and worship you*
Holy Spirit, the Paraclete, ... *I praise and worship you*
Free Spirit, ... *I praise and worship you*
Spirit of Adoption, ... *I praise and worship you*
Spirit of Judgment, ... *I praise and worship you*
Living Waters, ... *I praise and worship you*
Glory be ...
Continue to thanksgiving...

Thanksgiving Prayers

For the gift of life...*Jesus, I thank you*

For the gift of freewill... *Jesus, I thank you*

For the gift of my Christian faith...*Jesus, I thank you*

For giving me hope each day...*Jesus, I thank you*

For the gift of a home...*Jesus, I thank you*

For my parents, ... *Jesus, I thank you*

For my family members (name them)... *Jesus, I thank you*

For the gift of my education...*Jesus, I thank you*

For the gift of my job/business... *Jesus, I thank you*

For the gift of my health... *Jesus, I thank you*

For the gift of a sound mind, wisdom, and knowledge...*Jesus, I thank you*

For financial security in the family... *Jesus, I thank you*

For love, joy, and peace in my family...*Jesus, I thank you*

For our friends, acquaintances, and extended family... *Jesus, I thank you*

For our daily bread...*Jesus, I thank you*

For our family vehicle(s)... *Jesus, I thank you*

For my natural gifts and talents ...*Jesus, I thank you*

For the good sleep each night ... *Jesus, I thank you*

For protecting me each day ...*Jesus, I thank you*

For all the help I received from others... *Jesus, I thank you*

For purifying me through my sufferings...*Jesus, I thank you*

For forgiving my sins... *Jesus, I thank you*

For keeping me away from sin and evil... *Jesus, I thank you*

For saving me from hell and eternal damnation... *Jesus, I thank you*

For dying for me...*Jesus, I thank you*

For loving me... *Jesus, I thank you*

For knowing me and caring for me...*Jesus, I thank you*

For the plans you have for me...*Jesus, I thank you*

For choosing my vocation, career, and ministry...*Jesus, I thank you*

For hearing and answering my prayers...*Jesus, I thank you*

For healing me...*Jesus, I thank you*

For blessing me... *Jesus, I thank you*

For using me for your kingdom...*Jesus, I thank you*

For guiding me... *Jesus, I thank you*

For the gift of heaven and eternal life ...*Jesus, I thank you*

For watching over me and my family... *Jesus, I thank you*

For meeting all my needs... *Jesus, I thank you*

Glory be...

Continue to repentance...

Repentance of Sins

For the sin of idolatry, ... Jesus have mercy on me and forgive me

For the sin of disobedience, ... Jesus have mercy on me and forgive me

For the sin of stubbornness, ... Jesus have mercy on me and forgive me

For the sin of rebelliousness, ... Jesus have mercy on me and forgive me

For the sin of blasphemy, ... Jesus have mercy on me and forgive me

For the sin of unbelief, ... Jesus have mercy on me and forgive me

For not praying every day, ... Jesus have mercy on me and forgive me

For not reading the Bible every day, ... Jesus have mercy on me and forgive me

For my superstitious beliefs, ... Jesus have mercy on me and forgive me

For engaging in occult activities, ... Jesus have mercy on me and forgive me

For loving anything more than you, ... Jesus have mercy on me and forgive me

For taking the Lord's name in vain, ... Jesus have mercy on me and forgive me

For not using my talents for the glory of God, ... Jesus have mercy on me and forgive me

For profaning the Lord's day, ... Jesus have mercy on me and forgive me

For missing Mass on Sundays, ... Jesus have mercy on me and forgive me

For dishonoring my parents, ... *Jesus have mercy on me and forgive me*

For not loving others unconditionally, ... *Jesus have mercy on me and forgive me*

For the sin of abortion, ... *Jesus have mercy on me and forgive me*

For the sin of murder, ... *Jesus have mercy on me and forgive me*

For the sin of racism, ... *Jesus have mercy on me and forgive me*

For the sin of discrimination and favoritism, ... *Jesus have mercy on me and forgive me*

For the sin of smoking, ... *Jesus have mercy on me and forgive me*

For the sin of alcohol addiction, ...*Jesus have mercy on me and forgive me*

For the sin of drug addiction, ...*Jesus have mercy on me and forgive me*

For the sins of the flesh, ...*Jesus have mercy on me and forgive me*

For being worldly, ...Jesus have mercy on me and forgive me

For wasting or misusing time, ...Jesus have mercy on me and forgive me

For entertaining wrong desires, ...Jesus have mercy on me and forgive me

For not tithing, ...Jesus have mercy on me and forgive me

For being stingy and miserly, ...Jesus have mercy on me and forgive me

For living lavishly and wasting money, ...Jesus have mercy on me and forgive me

For the sin of lying, ...Jesus have mercy on me and forgive me

For the sin of boasting, ...Jesus have mercy on me and forgive me

For the sin of gossiping, ...Jesus have mercy on me and forgive me

For the sin of false accusation, ...Jesus have mercy on me and forgive me

For the sin of false witnessing, ...Jesus have mercy on me and forgive me

For not helping the poor, ...Jesus have mercy on me and forgive me

For coveting others' property, ...Jesus have mercy on me and forgive me

For desiring what is not mine, …Jesus have mercy on me and forgive me

For the sin of pride, …Jesus have mercy on me and forgive me

For the sin of envy, …Jesus have mercy on me and forgive me

For the sin of anger, …Jesus have mercy on me and forgive me

For the sin of sloth, …Jesus have mercy on me and forgive me

For the sin of lust, …Jesus have mercy on me and forgive me

For the sin of gluttony, …Jesus have mercy on me and forgive me

For the sin of greed, …Jesus have mercy on me and forgive me

For all my hidden sins, …Jesus have mercy on me and forgive me

For sins of omission, …Jesus have mercy on me and forgive me

For my sinful thoughts, …Jesus have mercy on me and forgive me

For my sinful words, …Jesus have mercy on me and forgive me

For my sinful actions, …Jesus have mercy on me and forgive me

Glory be …

Continue to forgiveness…

Forgiveness

All those who mocked me, ...*Jesus, I forgive*
All those who rejected me, ...*Jesus, I forgive*
All those who hate me, ...*Jesus, I forgive*
All those who hurt me physically, ...*Jesus, I forgive*
All those who hurt me emotionally, ... *Jesus, I forgive*
All those who condemned me, ...*Jesus, I forgive*
All those who misunderstood me, ...*Jesus, I forgive*
All those who discriminated me, ...*Jesus, I forgive*
All those who cheated me, ... *Jesus, I forgive*
All those who abused me, ... *Jesus, I forgive*
All those who ignored me, ...*Jesus, I forgive*
All those who neglected me, ...*Jesus, I forgive*
All those who slandered me, ...*Jesus, I forgive*
All those who abandoned me, ... *Jesus, I forgive*
All those who deceived me, ... *Jesus, I forgive*
All those who conspired against me, ... *Jesus, I forgive*
All those who stole from me, ... *Jesus, I forgive*
All those who gossiped against me, ...*Jesus, I forgive*
All those who falsely accused me, ...*Jesus, I forgive*
All those who treat me as enemies, ...*Jesus, I forgive*
For all the sins that my parents committed against me, ...*Jesus, I forgive*
For all the sins that my spouse committed against me, ...*Jesus, I forgive*
For all the sins that my children committed against me, ...*Jesus, I forgive*
For all the sins that my friends committed against me, ...*Jesus, I forgive*
For all sins that my coworkers committed against me, ...*Jesus, I forgive*

15

For all the sins that my superiors committed against me, ...*Jesus, I forgive*

For all the sins that the Church (religious people) committed against me, ...*Jesus, I forgive*...

Glory be...

Prayer for enemies

Jesus have mercy on my enemies, ... *and bless them*

Jesus have mercy on those who hate me, ... *and bless them*

Jesus have mercy on those who abuse me, ... *and bless them*

Jesus have mercy on all who persecute me, ... *and bless them*

Jesus have mercy on all who cheated me, ... *and bless them*

Jesus have mercy on all who ignore me, ... *and bless them*

Jesus have mercy on all who plot and conspire against me, ... *and bless them*

Jesus have mercy on those who mocked me, ... *and bless them*

Jesus have mercy on those who discriminate me, ... *and bless them*

Jesus have mercy on those who hurt me, ... *and bless them*

Jesus have mercy on those who rejected me, ... *and bless them*

Jesus have mercy on those who slandered against me, ... *and bless them*

Jesus have mercy on those who rejoiced at my downfall, ... *and bless them*

Jesus have mercy on those who maligned me, ... *and bless them*

Jesus have mercy on those who obstructed my success, ... *and bless them*

Jesus have mercy on those who betrayed me, ... *and bless them*

Jesus have mercy on those who insulted me, ... *and bless them*

Jesus have mercy on those who spread falsehood about me, ... *and bless them.* ...

Glory be...

Continue to faith...

16

Protection

From all dangers, ... *Jesus, protect our family*
From accidents and injuries, ... *Jesus, protect our family*
From natural calamities, ... *Jesus, protect our family*
From people who tempt us to sin, ... *Jesus, protect our family*
From scandals and controversies, ... *Jesus, protect our family*
From unforeseen illnesses, ... *Jesus, protect our family*
From unexpected bills and expenditures, ... *Jesus, protect our family*
During our weak moments, ... *Jesus, protect our family*
From the consequences of wrong decisions, ... *Jesus, protect our family*
From the consequences of our sins, ... *Jesus, protect our family*
From all evil spiritual forces and demons, ... *Jesus, protect our family*
From the plans of Satan, ... *Jesus, protect our family*
From the lies of the devil, ... *Jesus, protect our family*
From the deceptions of Satan, ... *Jesus, protect our family*
From evil and wicked people, ... *Jesus, protect our family*
From curses and spells, ... *Jesus, protect our family*
From sinful people, ... *Jesus, protect our family*
From all air, water borne, and food related illnesses, ... *Jesus, protect our family*
From all fights, arguments, and divisions, ... *Jesus, protect our family*
From sinful thoughts and inclinations, ... *Jesus, protect our family*

Jesus, protect my spouse,... *and keep him/her safe*
Jesus, protect our children,... *and keep them safe*
Jesus, protect our parents,... *and keep them safe*

17

Jesus, protect our siblings,... *and keep them safe*
Jesus, protect all our family members,... *and keep them safe*
Jesus, protect all our friends and well wishers,... *and keep them safe*
Jesus protect all our workmates,... *and keep them safe*
Jesus protect all our prayer group members,... *and keep them safe*
Jesus protect all the religious,... *and keep them safe*
Glory be...

Sealing Prayer
We cover our family, ... *with the cross of Jesus*
We cover our family, ... *with the wounds of Jesus*
We cover our family, ... *with the blood of Jesus*
We cover our family, ... *with the light of Jesus*
We cover our family, ... *with the love of Jesus*
We cover our family, ... *with the mercy of Jesus*
We cover our family, ... *with the spirit of Jesus*
We cover our family, ... *with the grace of Jesus*
We cover our family, ... *with the truth of Jesus*
We cover our family, ... *with the righteousness of Jesus*
We cover our family, ... *with the shield of faith*
We cover our family, ... *with the helmet of salvation*
We cover our family, ... *with the shoes of peace*
We cover our family, ... *with the belt of truth*
We cover our family, ... *with the sword of the Spirit, the word of God*
Glory be...

Psalm 91 (God's promise of protection)

He who dwells in the secret place of the most High shall abide under the shadow of the Almighty, will say of the Lord, He is my refuge and my fortress: my God; in him will I trust.

He shall deliver you from the snare of the fowler, and from the deadly pestilence.

He shall cover you with his feathers, and under his wings you will find refuge: his faithfulness shall be a shield and buckler.

You shall not be afraid for the terror by night; nor for the arrow that flies by day; Nor for the pestilence that walks in darkness; nor for the destruction that wastes at noonday.

A thousand shall fall at your side, and ten thousand at your right hand; but it shall not come near you. Only with your eyes shall you behold and see the reward of the wicked.

Because you have made the Lord, your refuge, the most High, your dwelling place; No evil befall you, neither shall any plague come near your dwelling.

For he shall give his angels charge over you, to keep you in all your ways. They shall bear you up in their hands, lest you dash your foot against a stone.

You shall tread upon the lion and adder: the young lion and the serpent, you shall trample under feet.

Those who love me, I will deliver him: I will protect him, because he knows my name.

He shall call upon me, and I will answer him: I will be with him in trouble; I will deliver him, and honor him.

With long life will I satisfy him, and show him my salvation.

Intercession

Jesus, have mercy on the sick, ... *and fill them with your Holy Spirit*

Jesus, have mercy on the mentally ill, ...

Jesus, have mercy on the orphans, ...

Jesus, have mercy on the homeless, ...

Jesus, have mercy on the hungry, ...

Jesus, have mercy on the poor, ...

Jesus, have mercy on those who are oppressed by the devil, ...

Jesus, have mercy on those affected by natural calamities, ...

Jesus, have mercy on those who have lost a loved one, ...

Jesus, have mercy on those who are in danger, ...

Jesus, have mercy on those who are weak and are being tempted, ...

Jesus, have mercy on all those who are depressed, ...

Jesus, have mercy on all those with suicidal tendencies, ...

Jesus, have mercy on those who are suffering, ...

Jesus, have mercy on those who are in pain, ...

Jesus, have mercy on those who are bedridden, ...

Jesus, have mercy on those who are dying with terminal illness, ...

Jesus, have mercy on those who are physically challenged, ...

Jesus, have mercy on those who are hospitalized, ...

Jesus, have mercy on those who are undergoing surgery, ...

Jesus, have mercy on those who have met with an accident, ...

Jesus, have mercy on those who are tired and lethargic, ...

Jesus, have mercy on all those who are addicted to smoking, alcohol, or drugs...

Jesus, have mercy on all the atheists, ...

Jesus, have mercy on all those who practice occult, ...

Jesus, have mercy on all those who believe in superstition, ...

Jesus, have mercy on all the people of other religions, …
Jesus, have mercy on all the murderers and terrorists, …
Jesus, have mercy on all those who have committed abortion, and those who aid in abortion, …
Jesus, have mercy on all the thieves, robbers, scammers, and hackers, …
Jesus, have mercy on all those who do not pray or read the bible, …
Jesus, have mercy on all our enemies, …
Jesus, have mercy on all those who are worldly, …
Jesus, have mercy on those who don't go for Mass, …
Jesus, have mercy on those who don't confess their sins, …
Jesus, have mercy on all religious people, …
Jesus, have mercy on the Holy Father, …
Jesus, have mercy on our parish priest, …
Jesus, have mercy on all families, …
Jesus, have mercy on all marriages, …
Jesus, have mercy on all those who are divorced, or separated, …
Jesus, have mercy on all children, …
Jesus, have mercy on all teenagers, …
Jesus, have mercy on all old people, …
Jesus, have mercy on all childless couples, …
Jesus, have mercy on all families with financial problems, …
Jesus, have mercy on our president (leader), …
Jesus, have mercy on all the lawmakers and politicians of our country, …
Jesus, have mercy on all the world leaders, …
Jesus, have mercy on the media, …
Glory be…

Continue to petition…

Washing in the Blood of Jesus

Jesus, wash our family in your precious blood, … *and fill us with your Holy Spirit*

Jesus, wash our home in your precious blood, … *and fill us with your Holy Spirit*

Jesus, wash all our belongings in your precious blood, … *and fill us with your Holy Spirit*

Jesus, wash our vehicle(s) in your precious blood, … *and fill us with your Holy Spirit*

Jesus, wash our finances in your precious blood, … *and fill us with your Holy Spirit*

Jesus, wash our bodies in your precious blood, … *and fill us with your Holy Spirit*

Jesus, wash our organs in your precious blood, … *and fill us with your Holy Spirit*

Jesus, wash our minds in your precious blood, … *and fill us with your Holy Spirit*

Jesus, wash our hearts in your precious blood, … *and fill us with your Holy Spirit*

Jesus, wash our parents in your precious blood, … *and fill them with your Holy Spirit*

Jesus, wash our siblings in your precious blood, … *and fill them with your Holy Spirit*

Jesus, wash extended family members in your precious blood, … *and fill them with your Holy Spirit*

Jesus, wash our friends and well wishers in your precious blood, … *and fill them with your Holy Spirit*

Jesus, wash our plans, desires, and ambitions in your precious blood, … *and fill us with your Holy Spirit*

Glory be…

Continue to petitions

Petition Prayer

Jesus have mercy on our family, ... and fill us with your Holy Spirit

Jesus have mercy on our family, ... and fill us with your presence

Jesus have mercy on our family, ... and fill us with your love

Jesus have mercy on our family, ... and increase our faith

Jesus have mercy on our family, ... and wash us in your precious blood

Jesus have mercy on our family, ... and bless us

Jesus have mercy on our family, ... and fill us with your wisdom

Jesus have mercy on our family, ... and protect us at all times

Jesus have mercy on our family, ... and take care of our financial needs

Jesus have mercy on our family, ... and help us pay our bills

Jesus have mercy on our family, ... and help us payoff our loans

Jesus have mercy on our family, ... and help us save money for future needs

Jesus have mercy on our family, ... and help us avoid unnecessary expenses

Jesus have mercy on our family, ... and give us continuous source of income

Jesus have mercy on our family, ...and keep us healthy

Jesus have mercy on our family, ...and heal our sicknesses

Jesus have mercy on our family, ... and increase our love for each other

Jesus have mercy on our family, ... and keep us united always

Jesus have mercy on our family, ... and increase our respect one another

Jesus have mercy on our family, ... and fill our home with joy and peace

At this time, each family member can lift up their petitions.

Pray the Rosary

Recite the Holy Rosary as a family. How to pray the Rosary and why we should pray the Rosary in given in the second part of the book.

Continue to next page (Scripture reading)

Read God's Word

Read one chapter of the Bible every day beginning with the Gospels. Every one in the family can take turns. In the second part of this book, there is a section explaining the blessings we receive when we read God's Word. There is also a section on how to read the Bible and get the best out of it.

Closing

In the name of the Father, and of the Son, and of the Holy Spirit. Amen

Morning Prayer

In the name of the Father, and of the Son, and of the Holy Spirit. Amen.

Read Psalm 91 (Psalm of Protection)

Read Psalm 23 (Psalm of Provision)

If you have children, lay your hands on them, say aloud and claim these Bible verses.

The Lord bless you and keep you; the Lord make his face to shine upon you, and be gracious to you; the Lord lift up his countenance upon you, and give you peace. (Num 6:24)

In the Lord all the offspring of Israel shall triumph and glory. (Is 45:25)

My God will fully satisfy every need of yours according to his riches in glory in Christ Jesus. (Phil 4:19)

In the name of the Father, and of the Son, and of the Holy Spirit. Amen.

Part 2

Notes

Why should we pray as a family?

Jesus promised us that he will be with us
For wherever two or three are gathered in my name, there am I, in their midst." (Matt 18:20)

Jesus promised us that he will hear and answer our prayers
I say to you, that if two of those among you have agreed on earth, about anything whatsoever that they have requested, it shall be done for them by my Father, who is in heaven. (Matt 18:19)

We receive God's blessings
Praise the Lord, O Jerusalem. Praise your God, O Zion. For he has reinforced the bars of your gates. He has blessed your children within you. He has stationed peace at your borders, and he has satisfied you with the fat of the grain. (Ps 147:12-14)

You shall make an altar from the earth for me, and you shall offer upon it your burnt offerings and peace-offerings, your sheep and oxen, in every place where the memory of my name shall be. I will come to you, and I will bless you. (Exo 20:24)

We will grow in relationship with God
When the people have gathered together, men as well as women and little children, and the aliens who are within your gates, they shall listen so that they may learn, and may fear the Lord your God, and may keep and fulfill all the words of this law, and also so that their sons, who are now ignorant, may be able to listen, and may fear the Lord their God all the days that they live in the land to which you will travel, crossing the Jordan in order to obtain it." (Deut 31:12-13)

We pray for the needs of the family
He said to her: "Sarah, get up and let us pray let us pray and implore our Lord that he grant us mercy and safety." (Tob 8:4)

We grow in love
Let us be considerate of one another, so as to prompt ourselves to charity and to good works, not neglecting to meet together, as some are accustomed to do, but consoling one another, and even more so as you see that the day is approaching. (Heb 10:24-25)

Now I beseech you, brethren, by the name of our Lord Jesus Christ, that you all speak the same thing, and that there be no schisms among you; but that you be perfect in the same mind, and in the same judgment. (1 Cor 1:10)

We will be filled with the Holy Spirit
When the days of the Pentecost were accomplished, they were all together in one place: And suddenly there came a sound from heaven, as of a mighty wind coming, and it filled the whole house where they were sitting. (Acts 2:1-2)

Family prayer brings protection for the home
Because you have made the Lord, your refuge, the most High, your dwelling place; No evil befall you, neither shall any plague come near your dwelling. (Ps 91:9-10)

Family prayer and salvation
Believe in the Lord Jesus, and then you will be saved, with your household. Acts 16:31)

Family blessings
Blessed are all those who fear the Lord, who walk in his ways. For you will eat by the labors of your hands. Blessed are you, and it will be well with you. Your wife is like an abundant vine on the sides of your house. Your children are like young olive trees surrounding your table. (Ps 128:1-3)

Family prayer and financial blessings
Blessed is the man who fears the Lord. He will prefer his commandments exceedingly. His offspring will be powerful on the earth. The generation of the upright will be blessed. Glory and wealth will be in his house, and his justice shall remain from age to age. (Ps 112:1-3)

Family prayer teaches children how to grow in relationship with God
Guard yourself and your soul carefully. You should not forget the words that your eyes have seen, and do not let them be cut away from your heart, throughout all the days of your life. You shall teach them to your children and to your grandchildren. (Deut 4:9)

Why do we praise God?

Praise brings us into the presence of God
Enter his gates with thanksgiving, his courts with praise, and acknowledge him. Bless his name. (Ps 100:4)

Praise and worship fills us with joy and lifts our spirit
My lips will shout for joy, when I sing to you, and also my soul, which you have redeemed. (Ps 71:23)

They will arrive and give praise on Mount Zion. Then the virgin will rejoice with singing, the young and the old together, and I will turn their mourning into gladness, and I will console them and gladden them after their sorrow. (Jer 31:12-13)

Praise heals our inner wounds
Why are you sad, my soul? And why do you disquiet me? Hope in God, for I will again praise him: the salvation of my countenance. (Ps 41:5)

We acknowledge God's hand in everything by praising him
Bless the Lord, O my soul, and do not forget all his benefits — who forgives all your iniquity, who heals all your diseases. (Ps 103:2-3)

Praise lifts our prayers to God
I will praise your name unceasingly, and I will praise it with thanksgiving, for my prayer was heeded. And you freed me from perdition, and you rescued me from the time of iniquity. (Sir 51:11)

Praise is a demonstration of our faith (praise releases our faith)
They were walking in the midst of the flame, praising God and blessing the Lord. Then Azariah, while standing, prayed in this manner, and opening his mouth in the midst of the fire, he said:

"Blessed are you, O Lord, the God of our fathers, and your name is praiseworthy and glorious for all ages. (Dan 3:24-26)

The Holy Spirit comes upon us when we praise God
While the musician was playing, the power of the Lord came on him. (2 Kgs 3:15)

Praise removes obstacles in our lives
With all the people shouting, and the trumpets blaring, after the voice and the sound increased in the ears of the multitude, the walls promptly fell to ruin. (Josh 6:1-20)

Praise delivers us from evil
Praising, I will call upon the Lord. And I will be saved from my enemies. (Ps 18:3)

Healings take place when God is praised
Heal me, O Lord, and I will be healed. Save me, and I will be saved. For you are my praise. (Jer 17:14)

God intervenes when we Praise Him (miracles, wonders, healings, and blessings)
In the middle of the night, Paul and Silas were praying and praising God. And those who were also in custody were listening to them. Yet truly, there was a sudden earthquake, so great that the foundations of the prison were moved. And immediately all the doors were opened, and the bindings of everyone were released. (Acts 16:25-26)

Praise brings comfort in times of suffering
Give praise, O heavens! And exult, O earth! Let the mountains give praise with jubilation! For the Lord has consoled his people, and he will take pity on his suffering ones. (Is 49:13)

Praise strengthens us
Then they all together praised the merciful Lord, and were strengthened in their souls, being prepared to break through not only men, but also the most ferocious beasts and walls of iron. (2 Mac 11:9)

Why do we thank God?

Make every petition with thanksgiving

Be anxious about nothing. But in all things, with prayer and supplication, with acts of thanksgiving, let your petitions be made known to God. (Phil 4:6)

Be watchful in prayer with acts of thanksgiving. (Col 4:2)

We enter into God's presence with thanksgiving

Enter his gates with thanksgiving, his courts with praise, and acknowledge him. Bless his name. (Ps 100:4)

We worship God by being thankful to him

Since we are receiving an immoveable kingdom, let us give thanks, by which we offer to God an acceptable worship with fear and reverence. (Heb 12:28-29)

Our prayers will be answered when we are thankful to God

I will praise your name unceasingly, and I will praise it with thanksgiving, for my prayer was heeded. And you freed me from perdition, and you rescued me from the time of iniquity. (Sir 51:11)

Thanksgiving is a sacrifice (offering) that pleases God very much

Those who offer thanksgiving as a sacrifice honor me. Those who go the right way, I will reveal to him the salvation of God. (Ps 50:23)

We are called to be thankful under all circumstances

Give thanks in everything. For this is the will of God in Christ Jesus for all of you. (1 Thes 5:18)

Jesus thanked the father before raising Lazarus

Then, lifting up his eyes, Jesus said: "Father, I give thanks to you because you have heard me. And I know that you always hear me, but I have said this for the sake of the people who are standing nearby, so that they may believe that you have sent me." Jn 11:41-42)

Jesus was thankful even in times of shortage and lack
Then Jesus said, "Have the men sit down to eat." Now, there was much grass in that place. And so the men, in number about five thousand, sat down to eat. Therefore, Jesus took the bread, and when he had given thanks, he distributed it to those who were sitting down to eat; similarly also, from the fish, as much as they wanted. (Jn 6:10-11)

Ingratitude is a sin against God
He was entering a certain town, ten leprous men met him, and they stood at a distance. And they lifted up their voice, saying, "Jesus, Teacher, take pity on us." And when he saw them, he said, "Go, show yourselves to the priests." And it happened that, as they were going, they were cleansed. And one of them, when he saw that he was cleansed, returned, magnifying God with a loud voice. And he fell face down before his feet, giving thanks. And this one was a Samaritan. And in response, Jesus said: "Were not ten made clean? And so where are the nine? Was no one found who would return and give glory to God, except this foreigner?" (Luk 17:12-18)

Receive everything with thanksgiving
For every creature of God is good, and nothing is to be rejected which is received with thanksgiving; for it has been sanctified by the Word of God and by prayer. (1 Tim 4:4-5)

Be thankful amidst all suffering and hardships
Being strengthened with all the strength, in accord with the power of his glory, may you be prepared to endure everything with all patience, with joy, giving thanks to God the Father, who has made us worthy to have a share in the portion of the saints, in the light. (Col 1:11-12)

33

When it began to be light, Paul requested that they all take food, saying: "This is the fourteenth day that you have been waiting and continuing to fast, taking nothing. For this reason, I beg you to accept food for the sake of your health. For not a hair from the head of any of you shall perish." And when he had said these things, taking bread, he gave thanks to God in the sight of them all. And when he had broken it, he began to eat. (Acts 27:33-35)

Why do we repent?

Repentance makes prayer effective
Your heart was terrified, and you humbled yourself before the Lord, listening to the words against this place and its inhabitants, specifically, that they would become an astonishment and a curse, and because you have torn your garments, and have wept before me: I also have heard you, says the Lord. (2 Kgs 22:19)

Repentance brings healing
If my people, over whom my name has been invoked, being converted, will have petitioned me and sought my face, and will have done penance for their wicked ways, then I will heed them from heaven, and I will forgive their sins, and I will heal their land. (2 Chron 7:14)

If you truly amend your ways and your doings, if you exercise judgment between a man and his neighbor, if you do not act with deceit toward the new arrival, the orphan, and the widow, and if you do not pour out innocent blood in this place, and if you do not walk after strange gods, which is to your own harm, then I will live with you in this place, in the land that I gave to your fathers from the beginning and even forever. (Jer 7:5-7)

In their tribulation, they will arise early to me. Come, let us return to the Lord. For he has seized us, and he will heal us. He will strike, and he will cure us. (Hos 6:1-2)

Do not seem wise to yourself. Fear God, and withdraw from evil. Certainly, it shall be health to your flesh, and refreshment to your body. (Pro 3:7-8)

Repent and be baptized, each one of you, in the name of Jesus Christ, for the remission of your sins. And you shall receive the gift of the Holy Spirit. (Acts 2:38)

Repentance restores God's blessings
If you will return to me, and keep my precepts, and do them, even if you will have been led away to the furthest reaches of the heavens, I will gather you from there, and I will lead you back to the place that I have chosen so that my name would dwell there. (Neh 1:9)

The son said to him: 'Father, I have sinned against heaven and before you. Now I am not worthy to be called your son.' But the father said to his servants: 'Quickly! Bring out the best robe, and clothe him with it. And put a ring on his hand and shoes on his feet. And bring the fatted calf here, and kill it. And let us eat and hold a feast. For this son of mine was dead, and has revived; he was lost, and is found.' And they began to feast. (Luk 15:21-24)

Convert, each one from his wicked way, and make your intentions good. And do not choose to follow strange gods, nor shall you worship them. And then you shall live in the land which I gave to you and to your fathers. (Jer 35:15)

Repentance brings God's favor
Now, therefore, amend your ways and your intentions good, and heed the voice of the Lord your God. And then the Lord will change his mind of the evil that he has spoken against you. (Jer 26:13)

Why do we forgive?

Forgive others and God will hear your prayers
When you stand to pray, if you hold anything against anyone, forgive them. (Mrk 11:25)

Forgive and God will forgive your sins
Forgive your neighbor, if he has harmed you, and then your sins will be forgiven you when you pray. (Sir 28:2)

Forgive others and God will heal you
Forgive your neighbor, if he has harmed you, and then your sins will be forgiven you when you pray. A man holds on to anger against another man, and does he then expect healing from God? (Sir 28:2-3)

Unforgiveness gives Satan a door to enter our lives and torment us
Anyone whom you have forgiven of anything, I also forgive. And then, too, anyone I have forgiven, if I have forgiven anything, it was done in the person of Christ for your sakes, so that we would not be circumvented by Satan. For we are not ignorant of his intentions. (2 Cor 2:10-11)

Then his lord called him, and he said to him: 'You wicked servant, I forgave you all your debt, because you pleaded with me. Therefore, should you not also have had compassion on your fellow servant, just as I also had compassion on you?' And his lord, being angry, handed him over to the torturers, until he repaid the entire debt. So, too, shall my heavenly Father do to you, if each one of you will not forgive his brother from your hearts." (Matt 18:32-35)

To forgive is a command
You shall not hate your brother in your heart, but reprove him openly, lest you have sin over him. Do not seek revenge, neither should you be mindful of the injury of your fellow citizens. You shall love your friend as yourself. I am the Lord. (Lev 19:17-18)

Be kind and merciful to one another, forgiving one another, just as God has forgiven you in Christ. (Eph 4:32)

God keeps a strict account of sins of those who don't forgive others
Whoever wishes for vengeance will find vengeance from the Lord, and he will surely be attentive to his sins. (Sir 28:1)

The sacrifice of Jesus cannot help us if we are unwilling to forgive
If a mere mortal harbors wrath, who will make an atoning sacrifice for his sins? (Sir 28:5)

We should forgive unconditionally just as God forgives us
Bear with one another, and, if anyone has a complaint against another, forgive one another. For just as the Lord has forgiven you, so also must you do. (Col 3:13)

Always forgive
Then Peter, drawing near to him, said: "Lord, how many times shall my brother sin against me, and I forgive him? As many as seven times?" Jesus said to him: "Not just seven times, but I say to you, , seventy times seven. (Matt 18:21-22)

If your brother has sinned against you, correct him. And if he has repented, forgive him. (Luk 17:3)

Forgive and make peace with others before worshipping God
If you offer your gift at the altar, and there you remember that your brother has something against you, leave your gift there, before the altar, and go first to be reconciled to your brother, and then you may approach and offer your gift. (Matt 5:23-24)

Forgive others even if they are not repentant
Jesus said, "Father, forgive them. For they know not what they do." (Luk 23:34)

Make peace with all those who hurt you
If your brother has sinned against you, go and correct him, between you and him alone. If he listens to you, you will have regained your brother. (Matt 18:15)

Why we must seek protection from God

God is faithful. He will strengthen you, and he will guard you from the evil one. (2 Thes 3:3)

For you will not go out in a tumult, nor will you take flight in a hurry. For the Lord will go before you, and the God of Israel will be your rear guard. (Is 52:12)

You are my hiding place; You preserve me from trouble; You encompass me with songs of deliverance. (Ps 32:7)

But you, Lord, are my shield, my glory, and the one who raises up my head. I have cried out to the Lord with my voice, and he has heard me from his holy mountain. (Ps 3:3-4)

We need protection from evil and wicked people
The Lord is my rock, and my fortress, and my deliverer; my God, my strength, in whom I will trust; my shield, and the horn of my salvation, and my stronghold. I will call upon the Lord, who is worthy to be praised: so shall I be saved from my enemies. (Ps 18:2-3)

We need protection from sinful people
Keep me safe, Lord, from the hands of the wicked; protect me from the violent, who devise ways to trip my feet. (Ps 140:4)

We need protection from natural calamities
Be merciful to me, O God, be merciful to me. For my soul trusts in you. And I will hope in the shadow of your wings, until the storms passes away. (Ps 57:1)

We need protection from Satan and demons

God is faithful. He will strengthen you, and he will guard you from the evil one. (2 Thes 3:3)

We need protection during travel and driving

For you will not go out in a tumult, nor will you take flight in a hurry. For the Lord will go before you, and the God of Israel will be your rear guard. (Is 52:12)

We need protection for our home and belongings

The Lord is your keeper, the Lord is your protection, at your right hand. The sun will not burn you by day, nor the moon by night. The Lord guards you from all evil. May the Lord guard your soul. May the Lord guard your entrance and your exit, from this time forward and even forever. (Ps 121:5-8)

Why should we Intercede (Pray for others)

Intercession is our duty and obligation

So then, far be it from me, this sin against the Lord, that I would cease to pray for you. (1 Sam 12:23)

People are saved when there is intercession for them

When God overthrew the cities of that region, remembering Abraham, he freed Lot from the overthrow of the cities, in which he had dwelt. (Gen 19:29)

He said that he would destroy them: had not Moses his chosen stood before him in the breach: To turn away his wrath, lest he should destroy them. (Ps 106.23)

Have seven bulls and seven rams brought to you, and go to my servant Job, and offer these as a burnt offering for yourselves. But also, my servant Job will pray for you; I will accept his prayer, so that foolishness will not be imputed to you. (Job 42:8)

Intercession has the power to make God intervene in a situation

A blameless man, prospering, is to be entreated for your people, bringing forth the shield of your service, through prayer and incense, making prayerful supplication, he withstands anger, and so establishes an end to the necessary difficulty, revealing that he is your servant. (Wis 18:21)

I sought among them for a man who might set up a hedge, and stand in the gap before me on behalf of the land, so that I might not destroy it; and I found no one. (Eze 22:30)

Then Moses prayed to the Lord his God, saying: "Why, O Lord, is your fury enraged against your people, whom you led away from the land of Egypt, with great strength and with a mighty hand? I beg you, let not the Egyptians say, 'He cleverly led them away, so that he could put them to death in the mountains and destroy them from the earth.'

Let your anger be quieted and appeased concerning the wickedness of your people. Remember Abraham, Isaac, and Israel, your servants, to whom you swore by your very self, saying: 'I will multiply your offspring like the stars of heaven. And this entire land, about which I have spoken, I will give to your offspring. And you shall possess it forever.' "And the Lord was appeased from doing the evil which he had spoken against his people. (Exo 32:11-14)

God will bless us with spiritual gifts (and charisms) when we intercede

And while I was still speaking and praying and confessing my sins, and the sins of my people, Israel, and offering my prayers in the sight of my God, on behalf of the holy mountain of my God, as I was still speaking in prayer, behold, the man Gabriel, whom I had seen in the vision at the beginning, flying swiftly, touched me at the time of the evening sacrifice. And he instructed me, and he spoke to me and said, "Daniel, I have now come out to give you wisdom and understanding." (Dan 9:20:22)

Intercession can save people from destruction

He said that he would destroy them: had not Moses his chosen stood before him in the breach: To turn away his wrath, lest he should destroy them. (Ps 106.23, DRA)

Have seven bulls and seven rams brought to you, and go to my servant Job, and offer these as a burnt offering for yourselves. But also, my servant Job will pray for you; I will accept his prayer, so that foolishness will not be imputed to you. (Job 42:8)

Because Jesus set us an example

Christ Jesus who has died, and who has indeed also risen again, is at the right hand of God, and even now he intercedes for us. (Rom 8:34)

This man, because he continues forever, has an everlasting priesthood. And for this reason, he is able, continuously, to save those who approach God through him, since he is ever alive to make intercession on our behalf. (Heb 7:25)

Little children, this I write to you, so that you may not sin. But if anyone has sinned, we have an Advocate with the Father, Jesus Christ, the Just One. (1 Jn 2:1)

Jesus did not enter the sanctuary made with human hands, mere examples of the true things, but he entered into Heaven itself, so that he may appear now before the face of God for us.(Heb 9:24)

There is one God, and one mediator of God and of men, the man Christ Jesus, who gave himself as a redemption for all, as a testimony in its proper time. (1 Tim 2:5-6)

Intercession can heal people

A prayer of faith will save the infirm, and the Lord will alleviate him. And if he has sins, these will be forgiven him. Therefore, confess your sins to one another, and pray for one another, so that you may be saved. For the unremitting prayer of a just person prevails over many things. (Jas 5:15-16)

Then it happened that the father of Publius lay ill with a fever and with dysentery. Paul entered to him, and when he had prayed and had laid his hands on him, he saved him. (Acts 28:8)

Then when Abraham prayed, God healed Abimelech and his wife, and his handmaids, and they gave birth. For the Lord had closed every womb of the house of Abimelech, because of Sarah, the wife of Abraham. (Gen 20:17-18)

Hezekiah prayed for them, saying: "The good Lord will be forgiving to all who, with their whole heart, seek the Lord, the God of their fathers. And he will not impute it to them, though they have not been sanctified." And the Lord heeded him, and healed the people. (2 Chron 30:18-19)

What should we pray for (petitions)

Pray for God's presence in the family
One thing I asked of the Lord, that will I seek after: to live in the house of the Lord all the days of my life, to behold the beauty of the Lord, and to inquire in his temple. (Ps 27:4)

Pray for Wisdom in all matters (finances, decision making)
For if you would call upon wisdom and bend your heart to prudence, if you will seek her like money, and dig for her as if for treasure, then you will understand the fear of the Lord, and you will discover the knowledge of God. (Pro 2:3-5)

Pray for love in the family
But may God our Father himself, and our Lord Jesus Christ, direct our way to you. And may the Lord multiply you, and make you abound in your love toward one another and toward all. (1 Thes 3:11-12)

Pray for the Holy Spirit
Ask, and it shall be given to you. Seek, and you shall find. Knock, and it shall be opened to you. For everyone who asks, receives; and whoever seeks, finds; and to anyone who knocks, it will be opened. (Matt 7:7-8)

Pray for faith in all family members
The Apostles said to the Lord, "Increase our faith." (Luk 17:5)

Pray for your needs (petitions)
Be anxious about nothing. But in all things, with prayer and supplication, with acts of thanksgiving, let your petitions be made known to God. (Phil 4:6)

Pray for God's mercy
Be merciful to me, O God, according to your steadfast love. And, according to your abundant mercy, wipe out my iniquity.

Wash me once again from my iniquity, and cleanse me from my sin. (Ps 51:1-2)

Pray for healing (mind, body, soul, and spirit)
In your infirmity, you should not neglect yourself, but pray to the Lord, and he will cure you. (Sir 38:9)

Pray before making major decisions
Therefore, David consulted the Lord, saying, "Shall I go and strike down these Philistines?" And the Lord said to David, "Go, and you shall strike down the Philistines, and you shall save Keilah." (1 Sam 23:2)

Why should we pray the Rosary?

- The Prayers of the Rosary are inspired from Scripture.

- We honor Mary as the Mother of God

- We recognize her as our mother

- We invoke her loving presence in our family and into homes.

- We meditate on the life and ministry of Jesus.

- We are invoking the intercession of the Blessed Mother each time we recite the Rosary

- We are invoking the protection of our Blessed Mother.

- We are seeking the intervention of our Blessed Mother.

- Our Blessed Mother will draw us close to Jesus and teach us to do His will.

- Rosary is a powerful weapon against Satan and his army of demons

Why should we read the Bible everyday?

The Bible is the Word of God
In the beginning was the Word, and the Word was with God, and the Word was God. (Jn 1:1)

The Word of God teaches us about Jesus (God)
You study the Scriptures. For you think that in them you have eternal life. And yet they also offer testimony about me. (Jn 5:39)

The Word of God gives us direction and counsel
Your word is a lamp to my feet and a light to my paths (Ps 119:105)

General blessings
He who gazes upon the perfect law of liberty, and who remains in it, is not a forgetful hearer, but instead a doer who acts. He shall be blessed in what he does. (Jas 1:25)

God's Word fills and satisfies our spiritual appetite
Man shall not live by bread alone, but by every word that proceeds from the mouth of God. (Matt 4:4)

God's Word gives us wisdom, knowledge, and understanding
By your commandment, you have made me wiser than my enemies. For it is with me for eternity. I have understood beyond all my teachers. For your testimonies are my meditation. I have understood beyond the elders. For I have searched your commandments. (Ps 119:98-100)

The Word of God gives us knowledge and conviction of sin
Knowledge of sin is through the law. (Rom 3:20)

We are filled with the Holy Spirit when we read the Word of God
Give heed to my reproof. Lo, I will offer my spirit to you, and I will reveal my words to you. (Pro 1:23)

In him, you also, after you heard and believed the Word of truth, which is the Gospel of your salvation, were sealed with the Holy Spirit of the Promise. (Eph 1:13)

God's Word saves us
Having cast away all uncleanness and an abundance of wickedness, receive with meekness the implanted Word, which is able to save your souls. (Jas 1:21)

God's Word heals us
Indeed, neither an herb, nor a poultice, healed them, but your word, O Lord, which heals all. (Wis 16:12)

God's Word gives hope in hopeless situations
Whatever was written, was written to teach us, so that, through patience and the consolation of the Scriptures, we might have hope. (Rom 15:4)

If your law had not been my joy, then perhaps I would have perished in my misery. (Ps 119:92)

By the Word of God, miracles happen
By the word of the Lord, he closed the heavens, and he brought down fire from heaven three times. (Sir 48:3)

And so, they remained for a long time, acting faithfully in the Lord, offering testimony to the Word of his grace, providing signs and wonders done by their hands. (Acts 14:3)

The Word of God fills us with joy and happiness
I discovered your words and I consumed them. And your word became to me as the gladness and joy of my heart. For your name has been invoked over me, O Lord, the God of hosts. (Jer 15:16)

God's Word brings financial blessings in our life
The Lord your God will cause you to abound in all the works of your hands, in the progeny of your womb, and in the fruit of your cattle, in the fertility of your land, and with an abundance of all things. For the Lord will return, so that he may rejoice over you in all good things, just as he rejoiced in your fathers: but only if you will listen to the voice of the Lord your God, and keep his precepts and

ceremonies, which have been written in this law, and only if you return to the Lord your God with all your heart and with all your soul. (Deut 30:9-10)

God's Word gives us power to overcome sin
I have hidden your word in my heart, so that I may not sin against you. (Ps 119:11)

I will always keep your law, in this age and forever and ever. I shall walk at liberty, because I was seeking your commandments. (Ps 119:44-45)

The Word of God breaks our hardness (Unbelief, Blocks, Obstacles)
Is not my word like fire, says the Lord, and like a hammer that breaks a rock in pieces? (Jer 23:29)

The Word of God can reach the innermost person and reveal us our inner nature
The Word of God is living and effective: more piercing than any two-edged sword, reaching to the division even between the soul and the spirit, even between the joints and the marrow, and so it discerns the thoughts and intentions of the heart. (Heb 4:12)

God's Word teaches, reproofs, and corrects us
All Scripture, having been divinely inspired, is useful for teaching, for reproof, for correction, and for instruction in justice, so that the man of God may be perfect, having been trained for every good work. (2 Tim 3:16-17)

We receive emotional healing
The law of the Lord is perfect, reviving souls. The testimony of the Lord is faithful, providing wisdom to little ones; the justice of the Lord are right, rejoicing hearts; the precepts of the Lord is clear, enlightening the eyes. (Ps 19:7-8)

We receive direction and counsel in life
The book of this law shall not depart from your mouth. Instead, you shall meditate upon it, day and night, so that you may observe and do all the things that are written in it. Then you shall direct your way and understand it. (Josh 1:8)

God's promise of eternal life when we read the Bible
This is the book of the commandments of God and of the law, which exists in eternity. All those who keep it will attain to life, but those who have forsaken it, to death. (Bar 4:1)

God's Word increases our faith
Faith comes from what is heard, and what is heard comes through the word of Christ. (Rom 10:17)

God's Word comforts us in our distress
This is my comfort in my distress: for your promises gives me life. (Ps 119:50)

Deliverance from evil
He sent his word, and healed them, and delivered them from their destructions. (Ps 107:20)

God's Word fills us with joy
I discovered your words and I consumed them. And your word became to me as the gladness and joy of my heart. For your name has been invoked over me, O Lord, the God of hosts. (Jer 15:16)

How to Read the Bible

Have a longing and desire to read the Bible
I rejoice at your word like one who finds great spoil. I hate and abhor falsehood, but I love your law. (Ps 119:162-163)

Make my teaching your longing and desire, and you will be well instructed. (Wis 6:11)

If your law had not been my joy, then perhaps I would have perished in my misery. (Ps 119:92)

I have rejoiced in the way of your commands, more than in all riches. I will meditate in your precepts, and examine your ways. I will delight myself in your statutes: I will not forget your word. (Ps 119:14-16)

Have a sincere love for God's Word
I meditated on your commandments, which I loved. And I lifted up my hands to your commandments, which I loved. (Ps 119:47-48)

How have I loved your law, O Lord? It is my meditation all day long. (Ps 119:97)

We should read and study God's Word in addition to listening to talks, preachings, and homilies
These were more noble than those who were at Thessalonica. They received the Word with all enthusiasm, daily examining the Scriptures to see if these things were so. (Acts 17:11)

Begin the day by reading the Bible
I rise before dawn, and so I cried out. For in your words, I have hoped beyond hope. My eyes preceded the dawn for you, so that I might meditate on your promise. (Ps 119:147-148)

Blessed is the man who has not followed the counsel of the wicked, and has not remained in the way of sinners, and has not sat in the chair of scoffers. But his will is with the law of the Lord, and he will meditate on his law, day and night. (Ps 1:1-2)

The book of this law shall not depart from your mouth. Instead, you shall meditate upon it, day and night, so that you may observe and do all the things that are written in it. Then you shall direct your way and understand it. (Josh 1:8)

It is necessary for us to observe more thoroughly the things that we have heard, lest we let them slip away. (Heb 2:1)

Give ear, O my people, to my teaching; incline your ears to the words of my mouth. (Ps 78:1)

I went to the Angel, saying to him that he should give the book to me. And he said to me: "Receive the book and consume it. And it shall cause bitterness in your stomach, but in your mouth it shall be sweet like honey." (Rev 10:9)

Study God's Word

A wise man will seek the wisdom of all the ancients, and he will be occupied in the prophets. He will preserve the words of renowned men, and he will enter with them into the subtleties of parables. He will search for the hidden meanings of proverbs, and he will become familiar with the mysteries of parables. (Sir 39:1-3)

My son, guard my words and conceal my precepts within you. Son, preserve my commandments, and you shall live. And keep my law as the pupil of your eye. Bind it with your fingers; write it on the tablets of your heart. (Pro 7:1-3)

Ps 101:2

Study God's word in a group (during family prayer, Bible study groups)
When the people have gathered together, men as well as women and little children, and the aliens who are within your gates, they shall listen so that they may learn, and may fear the Lord your God, and may keep and fulfill all the words of this law, and also so that their sons, who are now ignorant, may be able to listen, and may fear the Lord their God all the days that they live in the land to which you will travel, crossing the Jordan in order to obtain it." (Deut 31:12-13)

Memorize and repeat Bible verses
These words, which I command you today, let it be in your heart.... Repeat them to your children and talk about them when you are at home and when you are away, when you are resting and when you are working. Tie them as a sign on your hands and wear them on your foreheads as an emblem. Write them on the doorposts of your houses and on your gates. (Deut 6:6-9)

Write Bible verses and paste it in the house in different places
When you have crossed over the Jordan, into the land which the Lord your God will give to you, you shall erect immense stones, and you shall coat them with plaster, so that you may be able to write upon them all the words of this law. (Deut 27:2-3)

Read the Bible out loud
Blessed is he, who reads aloud the words of this prophecy and blessed is he who hears and keeps those things which are written in it; for the time is at hand. (Rev 1:3)

Until I arrive, give attention to public reading of scripture, to exhortation, and to teaching. (1 Tim 4:13)

Teach and share the Word of God with others
Let the word of Christ live in you in abundance, with all wisdom, teaching and correcting one another, with psalms,

hymns, and spiritual canticles, singing to God with the grace in your hearts. (Col 3:16)

These words, which I instruct to you this day, shall be in your heart. And you shall explain them to your children. And you shall meditate upon them sitting in your house, and walking on a journey, when lying down and when rising up. (Deut 6:6-7)

Be doers of the Word, not just hearers
He who gazes upon the perfect law of liberty, and who remains in it, is not a forgetful hearer, but instead a doer of the work. He shall be blessed in what he does. (Jas 1:25)

Everyone who hears these words of mine and does them shall be compared to a wise man, who built his house upon the rock. And the rains descended, and the floods rose up, and the winds blew, and rushed upon that house, but it did not fall, for it was founded on the rock. (Matt 7:24-25)

But to the sinner, God has said: Why do you discourse on my justices, and take up my covenant through your mouth? Truly, you have hated discipline, and you have cast my sermons behind you. (Ps 50:16-17)

Read the Word of God with Joy
You became imitators of us and of the Lord, accepting the Word in the midst of great tribulation, but with the joy of the Holy Spirit. (1 Thes 1:6)

I have acquired your decrees as an inheritance unto eternity, because they are the joy of my heart. I have inclined my heart to perform your statutes for eternity, as a recompense. (Ps 119:111-112)

I will rejoice over your words, like one who has found many spoils. (Ps 119:161)

Read the Word in its entirety. (do not tweak the Word for your own selfish advantage)

You shall not add to the word which I speak to you, neither shall you take away from it. Preserve the commandments of the Lord your God which I am teaching to you. (Deut 4:2)

How to Pray the Rosary

1. Make the Sign of the Cross

2. Say the "Apostles' Creed"

3. Say the "Our Father"

4. Say three "Hail Marys" for Faith, Hope, and Charity

5. Say the "Glory Be"

6. Announce the First Mystery

7. Say the "Hail Marys",

8. Say the "Glory Be"

9. Say the "O My Jesus" prayer

10. Announce the Next Mystery; and repeat the above steps (7-10).

11. Say the closing prayers (Hail Holy Queen, etc.)

12. Make the "Sign of the Cross"

Abbreviation

Gen-Genesis
Exo-Exodus
Lev-Leviticus
Num-Numbers
Deut-Deuteronomy
Josh-Joshua
Judg-Judges
Ruth-Ruth
1 Sam-1 Samuel
2 Sam-2 Samuel
1 Kgs-1 Kings
2 Kgs-2 Kings
1 Chron-1 Chronicles
2 Chron-2 Chronicles
Ezr-Ezra
Neh-Nehemiah
Tob-Tobith
Judith-Judith
Est-Esther
1 Mac-1 Maccabees
2 Mac-2 Maccabees
Job-Job
Ps-Psalms
Pro-Proverbs
Eccl-Ecclesiastes

Song-Song of Solomon
Wis-Wisdom
Sir-Sirach
Is- Isaiah
Jer-Jeremiah
Lam-Lamentations
Bar-Baruch
Eze-Ezekiel
Dan-Daniel
Hos-Hosea
Joel-Joel
Amos-Amos
Obad-Obadiah
Jon-Jonah
Mic-Micah
Nah-Nahum
Hab-Habakkuk
Zeph-Zephaniah
Hag-Haggai
Zech-Zechariah
Mal-Malachi
Matt-Matthew
Mrk-Mark
Luk-Luke

Jn-John
Acts-Acts
Rom-Romans
1 Cor-1 Corinthians
2 Cor-2 Corinthians
Gal-Galatians
Eph-Ephesians
Phil-Philippians
Col-Colossians
Tit-Titus
Phlm-Philemon
1 Thes-1 Thessalonians
2 Thes-2 Thessalonians
1 Tim- 1Timothy
2 Tim-2 Timothy
Heb-Hebrew
Jas-James
1 Pet-1 Peter
2 Pet-2 Peter
1 Jn- 1 John
2 Jn- 2 John
3 Jn- 3 John
Jude-Jude
Rev-Revelation

More Titles from Gifted Books and Media

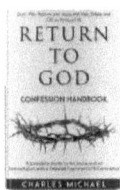

RETURN TO GOD
Confession Handbook

PREACHER'S HANDBOOK

GOD'S PROMISES AND BLESSINGS FOR AN ABUNDANT LIFE

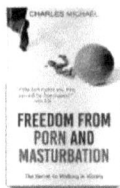

FREEDOM FROM PORN AND MASTURBATION

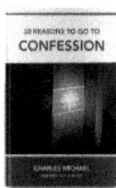

30 REASONS TO GO TO CONFESSION

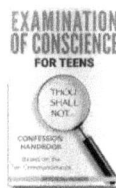

EXAMINATION OF CONSCIENCE
For Teens

EUCHARISTIC ADORATION
Prayers, Devotions, and Meditations

EXAMINATION OF CONSCIENCE
For Adults

SCRIPTURAL STATIONS OF THE CROSS

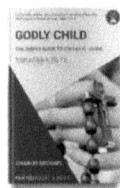

GODLY CHILD
Children's Guide to Catholic Living

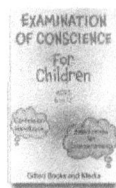

EXAMINATION OF CONSCIENCE
For Children

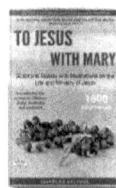

TO JESUS WITH MARY
Scriptural Rosary on the Life and Ministry of Jesus

SCRIPTURAL ROSARY
1000 Bible Verses

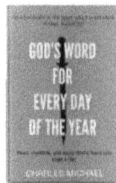

GOD'S WORD FOR EVERY DAY OF THE YEAR

SCRIPTURAL ROSARY BASED ON GOD'S PROMISES

58

DOWNLOAD THE APP AND PRAY ON THE GO

FAMILY PRAYER

FAMILY PRAYER

Download on the
App Store

FAMILY
PRAYER

GIFTED BOOKS AND MEDIA

www.giftedbookstore.com

60